W9-ASA-974

This book is dedicated to all who cherish America's history as a vast heritage of people and events—some heroic, some inglorious, but all part of America's epic struggle to come of age—and to all who know that understanding the past is essential to dealing with the present.

LINCOLN PARKS
THE STORY BEHIND THE SCENERY®

by Larry Waldron

Larry Waldron is Chief Interpreter of Indiana Dunes National Lakeshore and a free-lance writer. Among his publications are an award-winning book on the Indiana Dunes National Lakeshore and a children's publication on the Whitman Mission National Historic Site, Washington. Larry's longtime interest in the life and writings of Abraham Lincoln began at Willamette University, where he studied American literature and biology.

Front cover: Abraham Lincoln painted by Thomas Buchanan Read (note page 40). Inside front cover: Lincoln's writing box; photo by Bob Daum. Title page: Memorial Panel at Lincoln Boyhood Farm; photo by Bob Daum.

Published in cooperation with Eastern National Park & Monument Association

Edited by Mary Lu Moore; Designed by K. C. DenDooven

LINCOLN PARKS: THE STORY BEHIND THE SCENERY. © 1986 KC PUBLICATIONS, INC.
LC 86-81141. ISBN 0-88714-008-4.

Many free countries have lost their liberty, and ours may lose hers; but if she shall, be it my proudest plume, not that I was the last to desert, but that I never deserted her.

Some men are remembered by memorials that last long after their words and deeds are forgotten. Other men are remembered by stories of their words and deeds, passed down from one generation to another. Abraham Lincoln is remembered in both ways: by more National Park Service areas than any other American, and by words and deeds that will long endure—carved in our nation's memory, and carved in our nation's stone.

We know that President Lincoln freed the slaves, and saved the Union, and gave an immortal speech at Gettysburg, Pennsylvania. We learned these facts in our school books. But to learn the temper of the man, to take the measure of his spirit, and to chart the territory from which he rose, a visit to the seven National Park Service sites honoring Lincoln is in order.

Go first to the wooded hills of Kentucky and visit Abraham Lincoln Birthplace National Historic Site near Hodgenville. Walk past the Sinking Spring and climb the 56 stairs—one step for each year in Lincoln's life—to the memorial building sheltering a simple log cabin. It was in just such a one-room dirt-floored cabin that Abraham Lincoln was born. During his political campaigns much was made of Lincoln's humble origins. His father, Tom Lincoln, did not have history in mind, however, when he moved his family to Sinking Spring Farm in 1808. Like any other proud frontiersman, he was just providing a home for his family.

Travel west and north from Hodgenville across the Ohio River to Lincoln Boyhood National Memorial in southwest Indiana. Here Abraham Lincoln helped his father build a home in the wilderness. They felled trees for a cabin and planted crops. Mother Nancy and daughter Sarah cooked and sewed. Never-ending work was part of life on the frontier. If you visit Lincoln Boyhood National Memorial, you can watch men and women perform the same tasks today that the Lincolns did over 150 years ago. You can also visit the graves of Nancy and Sarah Lincoln. Loss of family from disease and childbirth was another feature of life on the frontier.

Drive west from the rolling hills and forest remnants of Indiana to Illinois and the prairie. In Springfield, Illinois, you will find the only home that Abraham Lincoln ever owned. It is now part of Lincoln Home National Historic Site. You can enter the sitting room where Abraham played

Preceding pages: In the 1930s Civil Conservation Corps workers in Indiana found the buried remains of a cabin on the old Lincoln farm site. Samples of logs and hearth stones were sent to Germany, where they were reproduced in cast bronze. Photo by Jeff Gnass

DAVID MUENCH

with his sons, never the least bit concerned that some townspeople considered them hellions. More serious business was conducted in the adjoining front parlor. It was here that a committee of Republicans notified Lincoln that he was the nominee of their party for the presidency of the United States.

Leave the Lincoln home and walk, as Lincoln did when he was in Springfield, to the second-story law offices he shared with Billy Herndon.

More than any other president, Abraham Lincoln symbolizes the American ideal of rising from the humblest of surroundings to the highest office in the land. From his birthplace in Kentucky to his boyhood home in Indiana (pictured here) to his parents' home near Decatur, Illinois, he lived in simple log cabins. As his fortunes improved, so did his dwellings. In Springfield, Illinois, there was a brown frame house. Next came the ultimate residence— the White House in Washington, D.C. Wherever he lived, Abraham Lincoln never lost the common touch of a man who had lived a third of his life in log cabins.

5

The White House during Lincoln's presidency.

From the law offices walk one block to the Old State Capitol where Lincoln delivered his immortal "House Divided" speech. Finally, go to the Great Western Train Station where on February 11, 1861, a crowd cheered Lincoln's farewell address as he prepared to leave for Washington, D.C.—and the presidency.

Trains still travel to our nation's capital, but whatever your means of transportation, you must make this journey in order to follow the last chapters of Lincoln's life. The White House has been home to 38 presidents (John Adams was the first president to live in it), sheltering the great and not so great alike. The man from Springfield brought unequaled intelligence and integrity to the executive mansion. Abraham Lincoln was burdened with as great a task as ever faced any chief executive: keeping whole the fabric of the Union while eliminating the stain of slavery. You can tour the White House where Lincoln lived and worked. You'll see the East Room, where on March 4, 1865, the optimistic chief executive presided over his second inaugural ball as the Civil War wound down. Only six weeks later the East Room sheltered the body of the murdered president.

Abraham Lincoln was one of many casualties of the Civil War. On November 18, 1863, he traveled to Gettysburg, Pennsylvania, to dedicate a cemetery to the Union dead. Make the trip yourself to Gettysburg National Military Park. Early in the morning, before the crowds come, stand on the knoll where the President delivered his brief address. Close your eyes. At first they are hard to perceive, but then Lincoln's refrains begin to ring.

*... that we here highly resolve that these dead shall not have died in vain—
that this nation, under God, shall have a new birth of freedom—and that government
of the people, by the people, for the people, shall not perish from the earth.*

The war was over when Abraham and Mary Lincoln went to Ford's Theatre in Washington, D.C., on Good Friday, April 14, 1865. As prospects were brightening for the country they were also looking better for the Lincolns. They sat close to one another, tenderly holding hands. But fate had a trump card to play in the person of John Wilkes Booth. If you visit Ford's Theatre National Historic Site today, you can see the reconstructed presidential box where the couple sat and where Booth shot the President in the back of the head. Then leave Ford's Theatre, walk across the street, and stand quietly in the House Where Lincoln Died.

You have now journeyed from the site of Abraham Lincoln's birth to the site of his death. There is one more stop. Across town from Ford's Theatre is the Lincoln Memorial. Here sits Lincoln carved from marble, 19 feet tall and larger than life, just like the man. Our tour has ended, and you have seen the strengths of our country's institutions and the possibilities within one man.

The president's box at Ford's Theatre has been reconstructed to look the way it did the night Lincoln was assassinated. Lincoln sat in the chair at the left with Mary to his right. Major Henry Rathbone sat on the sofa, the only original furnishing in the photo.

Lincoln the Boy

Tom Lincoln ducked into the warmth of a neighbor's cabin on Sunday, February 12, 1809, and shouted, "Nancy's got a boy baby!" Tom must have beamed with pride. Although just two days before he had celebrated the second birthday of his daughter Sarah, this pink, animated addition to humanity was his first son.

Thomas and Nancy Hanks Lincoln decided to name the baby after Tom's father, Abraham. There was more than tradition in this gesture. When Thomas was six, he was helping his father on their Kentucky farm when Abraham was shot from ambush by an Indian. Tom's older brother Mordecai shot the advancing Indian and saved the young boy, but it was too late to help the mortally wounded Abraham. Years later when Nancy Lincoln had her son, Tom Lincoln made sure his father's name was carried on.

The farm near Hodgenville, Kentucky, where Abraham Lincoln was born was purchased by his father in 1808. One of its attractions was a reliable water source called the Sinking Spring, recessed deep in the ground 150 feet downhill from the Lincoln cabin. The summer after Abraham's birth

DAVID MUENCH

When Thomas Lincoln settled here in 1808 the water source on the 300 acres he purchased was known variously as Cave Spring, Rock Spring, or Sinking Spring. Whatever the name, the spring provided refreshment for the Lincoln family, including the infant Abraham's first drink of water. Sinking Spring is a limestone sink typical of the terrain of central Kentucky.

Lincoln's birthplace is now a shrine, but once a simple log cabin stood here, abounding with the activities of the Lincoln family. In the spring Tom Lincoln would break the hard clay soil and plant his crops. Perhaps a more certain source of food was his musket, which provided the family with meat. At home Nancy would mend clothes and cook over the open fire. On nice days she would take baby Abraham out of the dark cabin to gaze upon the hills of Kentucky—the fifteenth state in a nation that would one day know Abraham's name from the Atlantic coast to lands not yet explored.

Nancy carried her newborn infant with her to the spring while she gathered water. There, in the cool recess of the earth, mother and son had a momentary respite from the summer heat.

Thomas Lincoln's background was well known. His Quaker ancestors had moved from Pennsylvania to Viriginia, where Tom was born. Then it was on to Kentucky. Nancy Hanks's background is less well defined. Like Sinking Spring, she had come to the surface briefly from sources unknown to nurture life and then depart.

After two years at the Sinking Spring farm, Tom and Nancy Lincoln decided to look for more fertile ground than the red clay hillside on which they were living. They found it ten miles to the northeast in the bottomland of Knob Creek. Abraham Lincoln later recalled, "Our farm was composed of three fields, it lay in the valley surrounded by high hills and deep gorges."

Here Tom Lincoln introduced his son to farm work. Early one morning Tom mounded up the fertile river-bottom soil; young Abraham followed, planting pumpkin seeds. But what the river gave, the river could take. The seeds and soil were washed away in a flood before they had a chance to germinate. It was only a minor setback, for the seeds were replanted. Not all losses at the Knob Creek Farm were so easily remedied, however. A second son born to Thomas and Nancy Lincoln died in infancy.

The Lincolns began to make a place for themselves in the community. Tom was appointed supervisor of the Nolin-Bardstown Road. The busy family had time for religious activities, too. While

An imposing structure shelters a simple log cabin. The cabin inside was moved from the Sinking Spring farm in the early 1860s. Its history prior to that is unclear. After Lincoln's death the cabin was displayed periodically around the country as the one in which he was born.

In 1904 the Lincoln Farm Association was formed, and by 1906 it had purchased the farm and cabin. The cornerstone of the Memorial Building was laid by President Theodore Roosevelt in 1909. The granite-and-marble building was dedicated in 1911 by President William Howard Taft.

at the Sinking Spring farm they had joined the South Fork Baptist Church. Because they disagreed with the congregation's support for Kentucky's legalized slavery, the Lincolns later joined the abolitionist Little Mound Church near their Knob Creek home. There were other problems with Kentucky law. Tom Lincoln had learned that through no fault of his own the title to each of his farms was in question. The family decided to move on to Indiana. As Abraham later remembered, "This removal was partly on account of slavery, but chiefly on account of the difficulty in land titles in Kentucky."

Abraham Lincoln recalled, "My earliest recollection is of the Knob Creek place." At Knob Creek Abraham helped his father with the chores and for a short period attended "ABC schools."

A 90-foot white oak was the last surviving tree to have lived during the Lincolns' time at Sinking Springs Farm. Known as the boundary oak, it helped mark the corner of their farm. The tree died in 1976, and the National Park Service is exploring ways to preserve the remaining 25-foot section of trunk.

The Lincoln home in southern Indiana was cut out of the wilderness. Measuring about 18 by 20 feet, the sturdy cabin housed an extended family of up to eight people. A reproduction of a pioneer home at Lincoln Boyhood National Memorial gives visitors an idea of how the Lincoln cabin appeared.

Frontier life demanded skills in woodworking. Thomas Lincoln was widely known as a carpenter and cabinetmaker. It was said in Kentucky that he had "the best set of carpenter tools in Hardin County." In Indiana, Thomas may have relied more on carpentry for a living than on farming. He and young Abraham helped build neighbor's cabins as well as the Little Pigeon Baptist Church. Several fine pieces of furniture fashioned by Thomas are preserved in museums.

Abraham Lincoln observed, "I was raised to farmwork." Though a hard worker, his quick mind became bored with the repetitiousness of physical labor. Books like Robinson Crusoe *and the* Life of George Washington *transported him to other worlds.*

In the fall of 1816 Tom made a preliminary trip to Indiana, where land was laid out legally according to a federal survey. He selected a wooded site atop a hill 14 miles north of the Ohio River. It was well into winter when he brought his family back to Indiana. They crossed the Ohio River on a ferry, landing near the mouth of the Anderson River. They arrived on Hoosier soil around December 11, 1816, the date Indiana was admitted to the Union as a free state.

To the west of their chosen hilltop was a reliable spring; to the north was Little Pigeon Creek. And all around were oak and hickory trees that had to be cut, first for cabin logs, and then to clear fields for crops. Abraham later said he had "had an ax put into his hands at once." Even as a child he was tall and strong, and trees fell with a snap and a rush as he wielded his ax.

Abraham was not quite so comfortable with another tool of the frontier—the musket. A couple months after the Lincolns' arrival, Abraham was alone in their newly constructed cabin. Outside he heard the bubbling call of a flock of turkeys. He aimed his father's musket through a crack and shot one of the birds. Distaste for this act of killing led him to recall years later that never again did he "pull the trigger on any larger game."

The Lincolns were not alone in the wilderness. When they arrived at the Little Pigeon Creek neighborhood they found a scattering of cabins. A year after their arrival the Lincolns were joined by relatives of Nancy's from Kentucky: Thomas and Elizabeth Sparrow and Elizabeth's nephew Dennis Hanks. On the frontier it was always comforting to have relatives near, and Dennis, though seven years older than Abraham, became his boyhood friend.

Even the cushion of friends and neighbors could not protect the Lincolns from all the dangers of living on a frontier. The wooded hills of southern Indiana harbor a deadly threat. White snakeroot, a tall flowering plant normally grow-

At Lincoln Boyhood National Memorial the living history farm recreates pioneer life of the 1820s. The farm features a replica of the Lincoln cabin, along with other hewn-log buildings such as the smoke house and carpentry shop. Costumed employees demonstrate daily chores like cooking and spinning.

The Lincoln family grieved over the loss of mother and wife. Dennis Hanks, with no family at all, moved in with them.

Dennis was not the only new resident destined for the Lincoln cabin. After a year of mourning, Thomas Lincoln returned to Kentucky and married an old friend, widow Sarah Bush Johnston. He brought Sarah, usually called Sally, and her three children back to Indiana. The other Sarah, Abraham's 12-year-old sister, had been making a valiant effort to fill Nancy's place. It must have been a relief when her stepmother arrived.

ing in shady areas, contains within its foliage a deadly poison. It is not a plant cows normally eat, but after a hot, dry summer such as that of 1818, they might have. When people drank the milk from such cows, they became listless, severely constipated, and got the "trembles." They usually died.

In September of 1818 first Thomas Sparrow, and then Elizabeth, fell ill. Nancy Lincoln went to their cabin to help. Perhaps at that time no one suspected "milk sick." Nurse and nursed alike must have drunk milk, normally a life-giving fluid. In this case it wasn't; both Thomas and Elizabeth died. By then Nancy, too, was suffering. She called her children to her bed. "Be good and kind to your father," she told them, "and to one another and the world." On October 5, 1818, Nancy died. She was buried on a knoll next to the Sparrows, a quarter of a mile south of the Lincolns' cabin.

Sally went right to work cleaning up the cabin and mending the children's clothes. It wasn't long before she had also mended the family. Lincoln later commented that "she proved a good and kind mother." Dennis liked her, too. In fact, Sally turned out to be the kind of person everybody liked.

It pleased Abraham's stepmother to see him read. While they were in Kentucky his parents had paid to send him to subscription schools. In Indiana, when he was 11, Abraham began walk-

14

BOB DAUM

When the Lincolns arrived in southern Indiana in 1816, they were surrounded by unbroken forest. Clearing the land was their first task. After 14 years they were farming about 20 acres.

ing a mile and a half south through the woods to a school near the heart of the Little Pigeon Creek community. At this school Lincoln later recalled that he studied "readin, writin, and cipherin." His formal education totaled less than a year.

Lincoln made the most of his "readin." In addition to the Bible, the most common book on the frontier, he read *The Life of Dr. Benjamin Franklin*, *Aesop's Fables*, *Robinson Crusoe*, and many others. Once when Abraham was reading *The Arabian Nights*, Dennis commented that the book was filled with lies. "Mighty darned good lies," Abraham replied.

It might have been the books Abraham read that made him a storyteller. Or maybe it was listening to Tom Lincoln, who had been entertaining travelers and neighbors alike ever since his son could remember. Most likely it was both. Whenever "Abe" got bored with physical labor he gathered the boys around and spun tales, tall and otherwise, to break the tedium.

One story Lincoln concocted gave evidence of a talent for satire that would prove effective later in his political life. On August 2, 1826, his sister Sarah married Aaron Grigsby. Sometime afterward when Aaron's two brothers got married, Abraham was not invited to any of the festivities.

In retaliation he wrote a satire on the wedding reception based on the Bible's fifth chapter of I Chronicles. The upshot of the story was that the bridegrooms had been given misinformation on which rooms in their father's house their respective brides were waiting in. The fictional results were, of course, uproarious.

BOB DAUM

Constantly outgrowing his clothes, young Abe may have pitched in to help his mother and sister on wash days.

Abraham Lincoln was only nine when his mother died in 1818. By all accounts she was a remarkable woman— intelligent, kind, and a loving mother. Her family buried her on this peaceful hilltop. Concerned citizens of Indiana erected the tombstone in 1879.

Death sometimes comes bearing flowers. Cows that ate the innocent-looking white snakeroot passed along a poison in their milk. "Milk sickness" brought death to many settlers, including Abraham's mother, Nancy Hanks Lincoln, at the age of 34.

Not quite a year and a half after Sarah Lincoln Grigsby was married, she died in childbirth. The 19-year-old Abraham was deeply affected. As he would do often in life, he turned to work to temper his grief. James Gentry, a local store owner, proposed that his son Allen and Abraham take a flatboat to New Orleans to sell produce and livestock. Just as books led Lincoln's mind away from the drudgery of physical labor on the frontier, the Ohio River led him away from his sadness to new, and sometimes frightening, experiences.

One night while they camped on the banks of the Mississippi River the two boys were attacked by seven black men from a nearby plantation. As Lincoln later remembered it, the boys "were hurt some in the mêlée, but succeeded in driving the negroes from the boat, and then 'cut cable,' 'weighed anchor,' and left." In spite of this incident they reached New Orleans safely. There these two boys from the Hoosier hills saw many new and wonderful things. However, there was a disquieting note at one location. Allen Gentry recalled that "We stood and watched slaves sold and Abraham was very angry. . . ." But he put the incident at the plantation behind him; Abraham Lincoln was not one to bear malice.

About the time of his return from New Orleans, Lincoln became interested in the law. He hung around courtrooms in Rockport, Indiana, observing cases and talking to lawyers and judges. A friend loaned Abraham a copy of *The Revised Laws of Indiana.* There he not only studied laws governing boundary fences and ownership of pigs and horses, but also the Constitution and Declaration of Independence. Abraham Lincoln was developing a mind that could encompass farce and fantasy, the cool logic of a legal code, and the elegance of our country's founding documents.

Finally the Indiana years were over. Sorrow at the death of both Nancy and Sarah still weighed heavily on the family. And John Hanks, Nancy Hanks Lincoln's cousin, had written of good land in Illinois. The family loaded their belongings into wagons. Abraham Lincoln walked alongside and guided one team of oxen as they headed west. He was leaving Indiana and his boyhood behind.

Today visitors to the Lincoln Boyhood site can experience what Abraham Lincoln wrote about in 1844.

> "My childhood's home I see again,
> And sadden with the view;
> And still, as memory crowds my brain,
> There's pleasure in it too."

The memorial building at Lincoln Boyhood National Memorial is Indiana's tribute to Abraham Lincoln's 14 years in the Hoosier State. The exterior features five bas-relief *sculptures depicting the major stages of Lincoln's life. Inside are a museum, an auditorium, and two memorial halls honoring Abraham and his mother.*

Lincoln the Man

Abraham Lincoln came to New Salem, Illinois, in 1831 as a young man of 22. Six years later when he left for Springfield he was a state legislator and a lawyer. In between he had worked as a shopkeeper, a farmhand, a captain of volunteer militia, a postmaster, and a surveyor.

BOB DAUM

Tom Lincoln selected a farm site near Decatur, Illinois, at the junction of timberland and prairie. Abraham helped by plowing the ground and splitting rails. Yet the lure of river travel once again drew the young man away from farm work. Abraham, along with his stepbrother John Johnston and cousin John Hanks, "hired themselves to Denton Offutt to take a flatboat from Beardstown, Illinois, to New Orleans; and for that purpose were to join him—Offutt—at Springfield, Illinois, . . ."

When the men got to Springfield they found Offutt drinking in a tavern. Worse than that, he hadn't built the flatboat. For $12 a month the three men agreed to cut the trees and build the boat themselves. By late April the flatboat had been completed and the three, along with Offutt, cast off down the Sangamon River toward the Illinois River and eventually the Mississippi. But they hadn't counted on James Rutledge's dam.

In 1828 Rutledge had built a cabin on a bluff overlooking the Sangamon River. The next year he built a dam for a gristmill and laid out a town on a ridge. He and his partner called the town New Salem. The dam held back water just fine; it also hung up the flatboat when Abraham Lincoln and his friends came along in 1831! A crowd gathered as Abraham took charge. He directed the others to shift the load and bore drain holes in the boat. The "fix" worked, and to the cheers of the onlookers the boat slipped over the dam.

Lincoln and Offutt were impressed with the friendliness of the townspeople, and Offutt was impressed with Lincoln. The merchant returned to New Salem after the river trip and opened a store. Abraham worked as his clerk. The store was a gathering place for the young men of the community, and Lincoln had many a chance to show off his storytelling ability. He also had a chance to exhibit another, less social, skill. Offutt had observed his clerk's great strength in hoist-

Henry Onstot's cooper shop is the only original building from New Salem's early days. When Onstot left New Salem for Petersburg in 1840, he tore down the building and took it with him. In 1922 the Old Salem Lincoln League returned it to its original foundation. Barrels built by Onstot in his shop were used by settlers to transport produce in their ox-drawn wagons.

ing barrels of pork about the flatboat. Now Offutt was boasting that Abraham could whip any young man around. Jack Armstrong took the challenge.

Armstrong was the leader of the Clary Grove "boys" from a settlement three miles west of New Salem. His boys gathered around as Armstrong and Lincoln struggled to throw each other into the Illinois dirt. When it looked as though Armstrong might go down, the boys jumped forward. Armstrong waved them off and declared a draw. Abraham became fast friends with Armstrong and his wife Hannah. He would visit the couple in Clary Grove to tell stories and play with their children while Hannah mended his clothes.

In less than a year Offutt's store began to fail, and Lincoln went from store clerk to soldier in the Black Hawk War. Chief Black Hawk was the leader of a band of Sauk and Fox Indians who had been banished to an area west of the Mississippi. In April 1832 when the chief led his band back to their homeland in Illinois, the state militia was called out and Abraham joined. The Clary Grove boys formed the majority in Lincoln's company and elected him captain. In 1859 he recalled that this honor was "a success which gave me more pleasure than any I have had since."

James Rutledge built his grist mill on the banks of the Sangamon River in 1828. By 1840 New Salem was a ghost town, but the mill continued serving farmers until it was torn down in 1853.

BOB DAUM

*At James Rutledge's tavern a weary traveler could
find overnight shelter and a meal for 37½ cents.
When Abraham Lincoln began boarding there in 1832,
he found a friend in Rutledge's 19-year-old daughter
Ann. Ann died in 1835. Lincoln, by nature prone to fits of
melancholy, was despondent.*

*Writers have built the story of Ann and Abraham into
a romance of epic proportions. The first account of the
romance was published in 1862 by John Hill in an article
meant to demean Lincoln's character. Two years
before, Lincoln had accused Hill of being a liar
on political matters. The truth about the relationship
between Ann and Abraham is as elusive as the morning
mist along the Sangamon River.*

Lincoln killed no Indians in the war. On the contrary, when one old fellow wandered into camp, Captain Lincoln saved him from bored troopers looking for their first victim. Lincoln did get to see the aftermath of battle when he helped bury five men who had been killed and scalped. This grisly task left an impression on Abraham, and he later recalled that ". . . every man had a round, red spot on the top of his head . . . and the red sunlight seemed to paint everything all over."

When the veteran returned to New Salem he had another battle to pursue. Before he had left for war, Lincoln had entered the race for the state legislature. As a Whig he stood for "internal improvements." That meant the building of railroads and the improvement of navigation. He was running against "the practice of loaning money at exorbitant rates of interest." And he was for education so "That every man . . . be enabled to read the histories of his own and other countries."

Lincoln wrote a letter to the local paper noting that ". . . if the good people in their wisdom shall see fit to keep me in the background, I have been too familiar with disappointments to be very much chagrined." As he seemed to have anticipated, he did not win, but he was pleased to have carried the New Salem precinct by an overwhelming majority.

Out of a job, Lincoln returned to a trade with which he had had some experience. He and a partner opened their own general store. The partner dipped into the whiskey barrel; and although Abraham did not drink, he spent too much time talking to customers. The store failed, and the two men were thrown into debt.

BOB DAUM

New Salem

In 1835 New Salem was a bustling frontier community, home to 25 families. Today it is an Indiana state park, saved from obscurity by the six-year residence of a gifted young man named Abraham Lincoln.

Frontier houses, businesses, and a school have all been reconstructed. Today you can tour the site and watch the blacksmith work, and you can visit the park museum. During the summer, plays about the life of Lincoln are presented in an outdoor amphitheater.

Failure didn't stick long to Abraham Lincoln. Even though he was a Whig and had run against a Democrat in the race for the state legislature, Democratic president Andrew Jackson appointed Lincoln postmaster for New Salem. Abraham guessed this position of postmaster "was too insignificant to make . . . politics an objection." He ran an honest, if somewhat loose, ship. One resident recalled, "The Post Master (Mr. Lincoln) is very careless about leaving his office open and unlocked during the day."

The job of postmaster did not provide enough income to live on. Lincoln earned additional income by splitting rails, helping with farm chores, and working at the grist mill. In 1833 he was offered an opportunity to be appointed deputy county surveyor. With the encouragement of friends he studied surveying and geometry books until late into the night. When he began performing his surveying duties, he was able to give an extra flourish to his postmaster position. He stuck letters in his hat and delivered them personally as he traveled the county.

Abraham's new career was almost cut short. Creditors sued Lincoln and his former partner over debts from their store. To reimburse the creditors the sheriff auctioned off Abraham's horse, bridle, and surveying instruments. Friends purchased the items and returned them to him. Soon afterward his former partner died, leaving Lincoln financial obligations to pay off over a period of years.

Life was not all work for Abraham. Early on in his New Salem stay he joined a debating society founded by James Rutledge. Members of the group did not expect much from this tall, awkward youth, but they were impressed almost at once with the force and logic of his presentation. The president of the debating society was of the opinion that all Lincoln needed was a little cul-

Lincoln's duties as a surveyor enabled him to meet many people—a real plus for a budding politician.

ture to be a success. In order to improve himself Abraham borrowed from fellow members an English grammar, the plays of Shakespeare, and other books.

For a while in 1832 Lincoln lived with Mr. and Mrs. Rutledge and their ten children. He began to enjoy the company of the Rutledge's daughter Ann. When the family moved to Sand Creek, Abraham frequently walked the six miles to visit.

Gossips have long speculated on the relationship of Ann and Abraham. Were they friends or lovers? That is a question we often cannot answer about those we know well. Without any conclusive evidence we can't answer it about these two young people. We do know that Lincoln was always very shy and uneasy around women. Ann died in 1835 from "brain fever." If she and her friend Abraham had a secret, it is now theirs to keep.

Lincoln was depressed by Ann's death, but he had a new job to keep him busy. In 1834 he made a second run for the state legislature. He took advantage of his travels as deputy county surveyor to campaign. At one farm he pitched in and helped with the harvest. The owner commented, "The boys were satisfied, and I don't think he lost a vote in the crowd." Some of the more educated voters had a problem with Abraham's backwoods appearance. That reluctance was usually overcome when they heard him speak. One doctor stated that Lincoln "knew more than all the other candidates put together."

Abraham's personality and speaking ability carried the day; he was elected to the statehouse in Vandalia. One of his fellow representatives was John T. Stuart, who had served with him in the Black Hawk War. Stuart, an attorney from Springfield, encouraged him to study law. Lincoln later described his legal education in an autobiography written in the third person. "After the election he borrowed books of Stuart, took them home with him, and went at it in good earnest. He studied with nobody. He still mixed in the surveying to pay board and clothing bills. When the legislature met, the law books were dropped, but were taken up again at the end of the session."

Lincoln was reelected to the legislature in 1836. During the following session he played a role in drafting and passing two major pieces of legislation. The first bill called for a sweeping program of "internal improvements" including a complex system of railroads and canals. Like the cargo on Abraham's second boat trip to New Orleans, the bill was a "pork barrel"; most of the improvements never materialized.

Lincoln was one of several Sangamon County legislators responsible for moving the Illinois state capital from Vandalia to Springfield. The cornerstone of the capitol building was laid on July 4, 1837, and the first legislative session was held in December 1840. In 1869 the old state capitol was sold to Sangamon County to be used as a courthouse. Almost 100 years later the state of Illinois repurchased the building and restored it to the days when Lincoln walked its halls.

The other bill was more successful. It transferred the capital of Illinois from Vandalia to Springfield. On April 15, 1837, Lincoln left New Salem and moved to the new capital. In addition to his legislative duties he had another job waiting. A month before, he had been admitted to the Illinois bar, and Stuart had invited him to be his partner. Abraham had come to New Salem with the skills of the frontier; he left with the skills of the statehouse and courthouse.

Even with his new status, Lincoln's arrival in Springfield was inauspicious. He rode in on a borrowed horse and went to the store of Joshua Speed to ask the cost of bedroom furniture. Seventeen dollars, he was told. The lanky attorney answered, ". . . cheap as it is, I have not the money to pay. But if you will credit me until Christmas, and my experiment here as a Lawyer is a success, I will pay you then. If I fail in that I will probably never pay you at all."

Speed looked at Lincoln and thought, "I never saw so gloomy and melancholy a face in my life." He offered Lincoln an alternative. "I have a very large room and a very large double bed in it, which you are perfectly welcome to share with me if you choose." Abraham inspected the room, dropped his saddle bags on the floor, and declared, "Well, Speed, I'm moved."

Not long after Lincoln arrived in Springfield he wrote a letter to Mary Owens, a woman he had met in New Salem but who was now living in Kentucky. "I am quite as lonesome here as I ever was anywhere in my life." He weighed the pros and cons of a romance between the two and ended with: "My opinion is that you had better not do it. You have not been accustomed to hardship, and it may be more severe than you now immagine [sic]." Mary took Abraham's advice and later rejected his offer of marriage because she said Lincoln ". . . was deficient in those little links which make up the chain of a woman's happiness."

JEFF GNASS

BOB DAUM

Though Lincoln never knew of these remarks, he wrote a letter to an older woman friend about his ill-matched love affair, observing that "Others have been made fools of by the girls; but this can never with truth be said of me. I most emphatically, in this instance, made a fool of myself."

Abraham had lost a sweetheart, but he was gaining a career. Stuart was a successful lawyer, and Lincoln soon began performing as a full partner. One page from the law partners' fee book in Abraham's neat and organized handwriting

Lawyers in the old state capitol worked on their cases in the law library. The table in the picture is from one of Lincoln's law offices.

Overleaf: The calm waters of the reflecting pool mirror the glow from the Lincoln Memorial. Photo by Jeff Gnass.

records payments to the attorneys ranging from $2.50 to $50.00. The fee book reveals that on one occasion part of a fee was waived when the client gave Stuart a coat.

Most of the cases the partners handled involved minor disputes over such things as property lines and unpaid bills. But in one early case Lincoln and four other lawyers defended Henry B. Truett, accused of murdering a political adversary. Working against them for the prosecution was Stephen A. Douglas, whom Abraham Lincoln was to meet later on a different stage. Lincoln was chosen to make the summation for the defense. Fellow attorney Stephen Logan noted that Lincoln gave a short but strong and sensible speech. Truett was acquitted.

In 1841 Lincoln and Stuart amicably dissolved their association, and from 1841 to 1844 Abraham practiced law with Logan. When Logan wanted to bring his son into the firm, Lincoln began a partnership with William Henry Herndon that would not be dissolved officially until Abraham's death. Lincoln joked that he had taken in "Billy" as a partner because he had supposed he had a system and would keep things in order, but that he was not much of a lawyer. Lincoln said he later discovered that Herndon had no more system than he did and that he was a fine lawyer, so he was doubly disappointed. As a result of this similarity of styles, the two lawyers had an envelope in the office marked "when you can't find it anywhere else, look into this." They also had a fine record of winning cases.

While Herndon would stay home and mind the office Lincoln would be out riding the Eighth Judicial Circuit. This was a traveling show consisting of a judge, a state's attorney, and assorted lawyers who visited 14 county seats throughout much of central Illinois. At each county seat they would stay for a week or so, trying the backlog of cases and dispensing justice.

Lincoln loved the circuit. He liked to travel across the bright, windswept Illinois prairie, so different from the dark and heavily wooded environs of his youth. But Abraham particularly relished the company of his fellow attorneys. At night they would sit around the hotel or tavern and swap stories. This was an art in which Lincoln excelled and he was highly admired for it. There was only one complaint his friends might register. When they hit their beds, flushed with drink, they were ready to sleep. Abraham, who didn't drink, often read late into the night by candlelight, his mind still whirring.

On one occasion while traveling the circuit,

Lincoln had the opportunity to repay a kindness he had once received. Hannah Armstrong, Abraham's friend from New Salem, was now a widow, having lost her husband, Jack. To make things worse her son Duff was accused of killing a man in a fight. Hannah couldn't afford a fee, but Lincoln took the case anyway. At the trial in Beardstown, Illinois, Lincoln carefully picked jurors he felt would be sympathetic. The jury heard the key witness to the murder affirm that by the light of the full moon overhead he had observed Arm-

The room and desks in the Illinois Hall of Representatives where Lincoln served as a legislator are a re-creation, but the memories are real. It was here on June 16, 1858, that he gave his House Divided speech to the Illinois Republican state convention. It was here also that his body lay in state the day before his funeral, held on May 4, 1865. Permission by the Illinois State Historical Library to photograph interior and artifacts from the Old State Capitol is gratefully acknowledged.

BOB DAUM

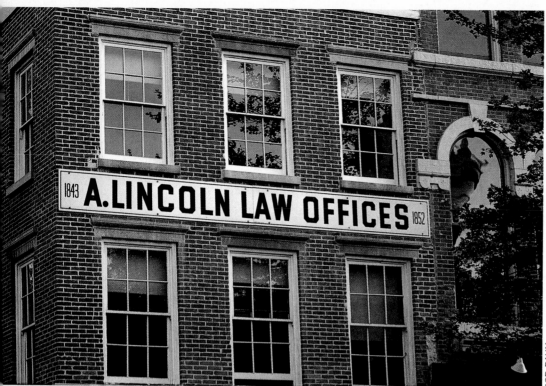

Lincoln had three different law partners and practiced in three different offices. He opened this office with Stephen T. Logan in 1843. From 1844 to 1852 he shared it with "Billy" Herndon.

strong striking the fatal blow. Lincoln coolly produced an almanac to illustrate that at the time of the murder the moon was just above the western horizon. Hannah was forever grateful for the resulting acquittal of her son.

Not all of Lincoln's cases were dramatic criminal confrontations. He also represented the Illinois Central Railroad and won cases limiting the amount of liability for shipments and exempting the railroad from certain taxes. The latter was a landmark case that firmly established Abraham Lincoln as one of Illinois's finest lawyers.

As Lincoln's fortunes in the profession of law were improving, so were his fortunes in affairs of the heart. In December of 1839, two years after he had arrived in Springfield, he met Mary Todd at a dance. She was pretty, bright, and vivacious—the product of a distinguished Kentucky family. Abraham was bright too, but shy and from a different kind of Kentucky family. Mary saw promise in this rough-looking lawyer, and a romance developed. Within a year they announced their engagement. Mary was staying with her sister and brother-in-law, who objected violently to the marriage. Lincoln was just "not sufficiently educated and intelligent in the female line."

Because of this criticism, and perhaps still feeling earlier hurts, Abraham broke the engagement on, as he later referred to it, the "fatal first of Jany. '41." He sank into a depression so deep that he could not attend to his affairs in the legislature. He called this melancholy condition "the Hypo," short for hypochondria. He was, he wrote Stuart, ". . . the most miserable man living. . . . To remain as I am is impossible; I must die or be better. . . ."

Lincoln got better and started seeing Mary again. He wrote to his friend Speed, who was now married and living in Kentucky. "Are you . . . glad you are married?" Speed replied in the affirmative. On November 4, 1842, Abraham Lincoln and Mary Todd were married. Lincoln wrote to Speed on March 24, 1843. "About the prospect of your having a namesake at our house cant say,

A visitor in 1860 called the Lincoln home "a modest-looking two-story brown frame house. . . ." When Lincoln paid $1,500 for it in 1844, it had one and a half stories. The second full story was added in 1856.

exactly yet." On August 1 of that year Robert Todd Lincoln was born.

The Lincolns were living in a boarding house when Robert was born. In the spring of 1844 they bought their own house for $1,500, and son Edward was born there in 1846. The boys brought great joy to the Lincolns, the father stretching out on his back in the living room, tossing the little ones toward the ceiling. If Mary Lincoln ever desired a gentle little daughter to love, it was not to be. Robert and Edward were followed by Willie

and Tad. The four boys were reared in a relaxed and undisciplined manner. Billy Herndon complained that when Lincoln brought the two youngest boys to the office they would "take down the books, empty ash buckets, coal ashes, inkstand, papers, gold pens, letters, etc., etc., in a pile and then dance on the pile."

Herndon didn't get along too well with Mary Lincoln either. She considered him a drunkard and a lout who was beneath Lincoln both socially and intellectually. He was one Springfield profes-

BOB DAUM

As his fame in politics increased, more and more people came knocking on the door of "A. Lincoln." One delegation of Republicans arrived on May 19, 1860, to notify him that he was their party's nominee for president. This doorplate on the home is a replica; the original is in the collection of the Illinois State Historical Society.

sional who did not grace Mary's guest list. But he had the last word in the feud when he published *Herndon's Lincoln: The True Story of a Great Life* in 1889, seven years after Mary's death. Although the book contains very interesting material on Lincoln's youth and career in Springfield, it paints an unfavorable portrait of Mary, based partly on Herndon's speculations.

Generally speaking, the Lincolns had a happy marriage. Mary had a biting tongue at times and a hot temper. Abraham weathered her occasional outbursts by retreating to his law office in downtown Springfield. When Mary withdrew to her room with migraine headaches, Lincoln was sympathetic and caring.

In 1846 the Lincoln family had a chance to see an unfamiliar part of their country. Abraham was the Whig candidate for the U.S. House of Representatives. By an almost 3-to-2 margin he defeated the Democratic candidate to become the only Whig U.S. congressman from Illinois. He took Mary and the two boys with him to Washington. At first the family was excited by the hustle and bustle of the capital, but with his heavy workload Lincoln had little time to devote to them. After three months Mary and the children returned to Springfield.

During the separation Abraham wrote to his wife: "When you were here, I thought you hindered me some in attending to business; but now, having nothing but business—no variety—it has grown exceedingly tasteless to me." He added, "Suppose you do not prefix the 'Hon' [for Honorable] to the address on your letters to me anymore. I like the letters very much but I would rather they should not have that upon them."

Lincoln's term in the House was highlighted by his opposition to the Mexican War. He thought the war "unnecessarily and unconstitutionally begun by the President of the United States." Back in Illinois he was attacked violently by Democrats and some Whigs for his stand against a popular

BOB DAUM

In January 1861 the Lincolns held a sale of much of the furniture and household goods from their Springfield home. Their new dwelling in Washington, D.C., came furnished. The Park Service has been able to include many of the original items in the restoration of the Lincoln home, including the dining table in this photograph. Other original items include a set of six side chairs in the front and rear parlors and Lincoln's shaving mirror in his bedroom. The only original bed is in the guest room.

war. When his term was over he did not run for reelection.

Shortly after his return home, Abraham's family suffered a tragedy. On February 1, 1850, Edward died, possibly of diphtheria. The death hit Mary particularly hard. She retreated to her room and hid her grief in darkness. A servant girl did the household chores, and eventually Mary found some solace in religion.

On December 21, 1850, Willie Lincoln was born; but life always remains true to its cycle of birth and death. To the east, in Coles County, Illinois, Tom Lincoln lay dying. Abraham wrote to his stepbrother with a message for his father. "Say to him that if we could meet now, it is doubtful whether it would not be more painful than pleasant." Tom Lincoln died without ever having seen his grandchildren, and Abraham didn't attend his funeral. Tom Lincoln had remained what Abraham Lincoln had moved beyond; perhaps the son did not want to look back.

After his term in the House of Representatives, Lincoln "went to the practice of law with greater earnestness than ever before." On the home front Thomas "Tad" Lincoln was born on April 4, 1853. Family and business had almost erased politics from Abraham's mind when in 1854 "the repeal of the Missouri Compromise aroused him as he had never been before." The Missouri Compromise had outlawed slavery from the northern territories of the Louisiana Purchase. The Kansas-Nebraska Act sponsored by Democrat Stephen A. Douglas would allow territorial residents to decide for themselves whether they wanted slavery. This doctrine was known as popular sovereignty.

In 1854 politicians opposed to the Kansas-Nebraska Act formed the Republican Party. Lincoln campaigned for the 1856 Republican presidential nominee, John C. Frémont. Frémont lost, but Lincoln gained exposure with his efforts. In 1858 the Republicans selected Lincoln as their candidate for U.S. senator from Illinois. His opponent was the Democratic incumbent, Stephen A. Douglas.

Lincoln kicked off his campaign with a speech on June 16, 1858. He spoke words that echo to this day:

BOB DAUM

The law library in the Illinois state capitol is where attorneys used to prepare their cases. After Lincoln became well known, law students would frequently ask to study with him. He replied to one, "If you wish to be a lawyer, attach no consequence to the place you are in, or the person you are with; but get books, sit down anywhere, and go to reading for yourself."

A house divided against itself cannot stand.

I believe this government cannot endure, permanently half slave and half free.

I do not expect the Union to be dissolved—I do not expect the house to fall—but I do expect it will cease to be divided.

It will become all one thing, or all the other.

BOB DAUM
BOB DAUM

Mary Todd Lincoln's bedroom (left) was connected to Abraham's by a wide door. The rocking chair in the foreground is an original in the Lincoln home. The kitchen stove (right) is also original. It was sold by Lincoln in June 1860 but was eventually exhibited at Ford's Theatre with other items from the house. The stove was returned to Springfield for display in the Lincoln home.

Douglas and Lincoln agreed to a series of debates during the campaign to emphasize their differences. One difference was immediately apparent. The 6-foot 4-inch Lincoln towered over his opponent by a full foot. Douglas did not wait long to point out other differences. He called Lincoln's House Divided speech "revolutionary and destructive." Lincoln accused Douglas of encouraging the "perpetuity and nationalization of slavery."

Slavery was the question of the day. Douglas insisted it was up to "the people to decide for themselves whether it was good or evil." Lincoln responded that Douglas "looks upon it as being an exceedingly little thing—only equal to the question of the cranberry laws of Indiana—as

something having no moral question in it. . . ."

Lincoln had no questions about the morality of slavery. As early as 1837 he had declared in the Illinois legislature that it was "founded on both injustice and bad policy." On August 21, 1858, before 10,000 people in Ottawa, Illinois, Lincoln reacted to Douglas's proposal for the extension of slavery by avowing, "I hate it because of the monstrous injustice of slavery itself."

Douglas accused Lincoln of trying to make blacks equal to whites in all respects. He said sarcastically, "I do not regard the negro as my equal, and positively deny that he is my brother, or any kin to me whatever." Lincoln responded that blacks were "perhaps" not equal in all respects, "But in the right to eat the bread, without the leave of anybody else, which his own hand earns, he is my equal, and the equal of Judge Douglas, and the equal of every living man."

The Democrats, and Lincoln, won the popular vote. But the final selection of senators came in the Illinois legislature, and there were enough holdover Democrats to return Douglas to the Senate by a vote of 54 to 46. The debates had given Lincoln national attention, however, and had set the stage for the last great chapter in his life.

In 1860 at the Republican Convention in Chicago, Lincoln was selected as the party's presidential candidate. Once again his Democratic opponent was Stephen A. Douglas. Because the country had been split in two by the issue of slavery, Southern Democrats ran their own candidate, John Breckinridge. As was the custom of the day, Lincoln did not campaign but let others tour the country making speeches on his behalf. His supporters popularized him as "Honest Abe" and "The Railsplitter." Rails he had split on his father's farm near Decatur were used as campaign props.

Lincoln defeated Douglas handily, 1,866,452 to 1,376,957, with Breckinridge collecting 849,781 mostly Southern votes. A fourth candidate, John Bell, running "on the Constitution" drew 588,879 votes. When news of Lincoln's victory arrived in the Springfield telegraph office, supporters cheering wildly and carrying torches filled the streets.

After the election old friends from New Salem, including Hannah Armstrong, came by to pay their respects to the president-elect. As Hannah told it, the "boys" started kidding her about the intention of her visit. She replied that not every woman has "the good fortune and high honor of sleeping with a President." The boys quieted down. Her real concerns were of a more somber nature. She was afraid Lincoln's enemies would kill him. "Hannah," he responded, "if they kill me, I shall never die another death."

Other visitors were more concerned with themselves than with Lincoln as Springfield filled with office seekers. According to Herndon, Lincoln gave them all the same answer: a story to chuckle over. Finally Lincoln had to hide himself away so he could write his first inaugural address. Then it was time to leave. On the morning of February 11, 1861, at the Great Western Railway depot he told his friends and neighbors, "To this place, and the kindness of these people, I owe everything." He felt that the task before him was greater "than that which rested upon Washington." After he had finished speaking, the train rolled eastward into the misty Illinois countryside.

Lincoln's Springfield neighbors ranged from working people to businessmen. This one-story house was originally located diagonally across the street from the Lincolns. Its owner was Charles Corneau, who ran a pharmacy where the Lincolns bought "caster oil," "cough candy," and "hair balsam."

Lincoln the President

As the presidential train wound its way across the country it stopped at various cities and towns so that Lincoln could address the assembled crowds. He had a serious problem to discuss. His election had triggered the secession from the Union of several Southern states over the issue of slavery. In Indianapolis he asked his audience, "What mysterious right to play tyrant is conferred on a district of country with its people by merely calling it a State?" What right did "one-fiftieth part of the nation in soil and population," have to destroy the Union? Lincoln hinted strongly that as president of the country he would "hold and retake its own forts and other property."

When Lincoln arrived in Washington he consulted with his newly appointed Cabinet on the draft of his inaugural address. Secretary of State William Henry Seward urged him to be conciliatory, "to soothe the public mind." The President agreed. When he delivered his address on March 4, 1861, he promised not to interfere with slavery in states where it presently existed; he would oppose for now only its expansion. He also pledged to support the law requiring the return of fugitive slaves. Although he made it clear that he regarded secession as "the essence of anarchy," he closed with an appeal for unity. "We are not enemies, but friends. We must not be enemies."

President Lincoln's words were to no avail. There was a Federal boil on the fresh complexion of the Confederacy. When South Carolina seceded from the Union in December 1860, Fort Sumter in Charleston Harbor remained in Union hands. Union troops at the fort had enough supplies for only 40 days. Lincoln needed to make a decision either to evacuate the men or to send in supplies and reinforcements. The majority of his Cabinet recommended against forcing the Confederacy into a hostile action. Deciding against these recommendations, the President announced that he would resupply the fort. On April 12, 1861, at 4:30 A.M., Confederate batteries began firing on Sumter. The next day the Union troops surrendered. It would not be the last defeat for the North.

Even in the midst of this developing crisis the Lincoln family had to make a home in Washington, in many ways a raw Southern town. Livestock wandered at will. Most houses had privies, and what sewer systems existed emptied into back lots and waterways. As for the roads, Mary Lincoln complained they were *"dust,"* which she presumed, "we will never be freed from, until *mud,* takes its place."

MATHEW BRADY—LLOYD OSTENDORF

Abraham Lincoln first visited Mathew Brady's photography studio in Washington, D.C., the day after he arrived to assume the presidency. In this portrait, taken there on February 9, 1864, he and son Tad are looking at a photo album.

U.S. LIBRARY OF CONGRESS

In honor of the inaugural of President Lincoln, a grand ball was held in Washington, D.C., on Monday evening, March 4, 1861, in a hall especially erected for the occasion.

Yet not all was grime and grit. There was a social whirl in Washington that Mary Lincoln very much wanted to be part of. Her first order of business was to redecorate the White House. It was in shabby condition when the Lincolns arrived. For improvements Congress had appropriated $20,000, which Mary quickly spent during trips to New York and Philadelphia. Unfortunately, in her eagerness she spent almost $7,000 over the appropriation.

When Lincoln found out about her expenditures he was furious. "It would stink in the nostrils of the American people to have it said that the President of the United States had approved a bill over running an appropriation for $20,000 for flub dubs, for this damned old house, when the soldiers cannot have blankets." Congress did vote the excess money, but Mary did not stop her spending sprees. Lincoln never knew of many of her bills, especially those for clothing.

Mary held fashionable receptions and entertainments at the White House. One newspaper described the First Lady as "our fair Republican Queen" and concluded: "Mrs. Lincoln possesses that rare beauty which has rendered the Empress of the French so celebrated as a handsome woman." Not all the reviews were so friendly. Many publications criticized her spending and even suggested that her fashionable dresses exposed too much flesh.

President Lincoln, too, suffered at the hands of the press. Southern newspapers portrayed him as Satan, prepared to destroy their way of life. Overseas the fashionable English magazine *Punch* ran a series of cartoons ridiculing him as incompetent. At home, Democratic newspapers belittled his proclivity for telling humorous stories. Lincoln didn't take criticism as much to heart as

Mary did. When late in his presidency someone expressed concern over one critical story he replied, "I have endured a great deal of ridicule without much malice and have received a great deal of kindness, not quite free from ridicule. I am used to it."

On February 20, 1862, the Lincolns' third son, Willie, died from a lingering illness. Mary was thrown into fits of deep depression over the loss. She visited spiritualists in hopes of communicating with her son. The President lost himself in his work: winning a war. He studied military tactics the same way he had studied law—by borrowing books, in this case, from the Library of Congress.

One thing the books apparently did not teach was how to pick a general. The first major battle of the Civil War resulted in a Union rout at Bull Run. This prompted Lincoln to place General George B. McClellan in charge of the Union's Army of the Potomac. "Little Mac" was a superb organizer, strategist, and builder of morale. He put together a 130,000-man army to march on Richmond, Virginia, the capital of the 11-state Confederacy. Unfortunately McClellan spent too much time preparing for war and not enough time fighting it. General Robert E. Lee and the Confederate troops were able to keep him from threatening Richmond. When the two foes did clash at Antietam, Maryland, on September 17, 1862, McClellan was barely able to defeat Lee in the single bloodiest day of fighting in the war. But contrary to Lincoln's expectations, McClellan did not pursue Lee, let alone destroy the effectiveness of his army.

The limited victory at Antietam gave Lincoln an opportunity to proceed with an action that he had been weighing for some time: issuing a proc-

In 1938 the veterans of Gettysburg gathered for a reunion on the seventy-fifth anniversary of the battle. A handshake symbolizes fruition of Lincoln's dream of a union once more made whole.

GETTYSBURG NATIONAL MILITARY PARK PHOTO

lamation of emancipation that freed the slaves. His Cabinet members urged caution. Secretary of State Seward had warned that if the proclamation was issued while the Union was losing, foreign powers would view it as an act of desperation. Six days after Antietam, President Lincoln issued a preliminary proclamation that would set slaves held by the Confederacy "then, thenceforward, and forever free."

Lincoln based his right to take this action on his powers as a military commander in chief. The proclamation would not free slaves in the border states of Kentucky, Maryland, and Missouri, as these states were not at war with the Union. The final proclamation was issued on January 1, 1863.

On the war front, McClellan still wasn't pursuing Lee. He wired Lincoln an excuse. Lincoln wired back:

President Lincoln replaced McClellan with General Ambrose E. Burnside. On December 13, 1862, Burnside led his forces against fortified Confederate troops at Fredericksburg, Virginia. Twelve thousand Union soldiers were killed or wounded in a disastrous defeat. Lincoln replaced Burnside with Joseph Hooker, even though the President worried that the new general might be overconfident. He wrote Hooker a fatherly letter that concluded, "And now, beware of rashness. Beware of rashness, but with energy, and sleepless vigilance, go forward, and give us victories."

Lincoln's wish for Hooker was not to be. In early May 1863 General Robert E. Lee attacked Hooker's army near Chancellorsville, Virginia. Even though Lee had only half as many troops, he was able to rout Hooker, forcing him to retreat across the Rappahannock River. When the President received the telegram bearing the bad news he cried, "My God! What will the country say! What will the country say!"

On June 28, 1863, Lincoln appointed a new commander, General George G. Meade. Four days later Meade was fighting the greatest battle of the Civil War. Fate had thrown Union and Confederate forces together near the Pennsylvania town of Gettysburg. The Confederate troops positioned themselves along Seminary Ridge, and the Union troops positioned themselves along Cemetery Ridge—a bizarre play on words. On July 1 and 2, Confederate soldiers and artillery assaulted Union lines. Then, in a heroic finale on July 3, 12,000 Confederate troops charged across open fields into a hail of Union artillery and small-arms fire. Some Confederates reached the Union lines, where blue and grey entwined in bloody hand-to-hand combat. The Federals repulsed the charge. Lee retreated, leaving behind on the battlefield not only the Confederate and Union dead but also his hope for a successful invasion of the North.

At Gettysburg the dead were hastily and inadequately buried. Pennsylvania citizens had successfully lobbied for a national cemetery, which

I have just read your dispatch about sore tongued and fatigued horses.
Will you pardon me for asking what the horses of your army have done since the battle of Antietam that fatigue anything?

was dedicated on November 19, 1863. After Massachusetts orator Edward Everett delivered the principal address, President Lincoln said a few words for the dedication at Gettysburg.

. . . we can not dedicate—we can not consecrate— we can not hallow—this ground. The brave men, living and dead, who struggled here, have consecrated it, far above our poor power to add or detract. . . .

It is rather for us to be here dedicated to the great task remaining before us—that from these honored dead we take increased devotion to that cause for which they gave the last full measure of devotion—that we here highly resolve that these dead shall not have died in vain. . . .

To ensure that the dead had not died in vain Lincoln needed to win the war and restore the Union. Meade, like the other generals before him, was not pursuing Lee to the President's satisfaction. This time Lincoln had a solution. In the west General Ulysses S. Grant had taken Vicksburg, Mississippi. Grant was a controversial general; tongues wagged that he drank too much. The President was only too familiar with the abundance of loose talk about public figures. "I can't spare this man," he emphasized. "He fights." Lincoln appointed Grant general in chief of all Union armies.

President Lincoln needed victories not only to win the war but also to preserve his political career. For the 1864 election the Democrats had nominated General McClellan as their presidential candidate. Fellow Republicans were discussing General Frémont as an alternative to Lincoln. To win the election the President was advised to withdraw the Emancipation Proclamation. "Should I do so," he answered, "I should deserve to be damned in time and eternity. Come what will, I will keep my faith with friends and foe." The Republican party kept its faith and renominated Abraham Lincoln.

With Grant in command, the Union army began to deliver victories. As part of a drive through the heart of the South, General William T. Sherman captured Atlanta. "My profoundest thanks to you and your whole army . . . ," Lincoln wired. General Grant was putting unremitting pressure on Lee's forces around the Confederate capital of Richmond. All these developments helped at election time. Lincoln polled 2,213,665 popular votes to General McClellan's 1,802,237. Among soldiers, many of whom carried a picture of "Father Abraham" in their knapsacks, Lincoln's margin was substantially greater: 116,887 to 33,748.

DAVID MUENCH

At Gettysburg on November 19, 1863, Abraham Lincoln began his speech with these famous words: "Four score and seven years ago . . ."

JEFF GNASS

Often fatalistic, Abraham Lincoln believed that death chose its own time and place. When Lincoln, flushed with victory in the Civil War, entered this ordinary brick building on April 14, 1865, he must not have expected that this was his time.

On April 9, 1865, General Robert E. Lee surrendered to General Grant at Appomattox Court House, Virginia. Though some Confederate forces remained in the field, for all practical purposes the Civil War was over. Lincoln's "just and lasting peace" had been achieved.

Now Lincoln could turn his attention to rebuilding the nation. There was also time to spend a night out with Mary. On Good Friday, April 14, 1865, the Lincolns, along with an engaged couple, Major Henry Reed Rathbone and Clara Harris, took a carriage to Ford's Theatre, where they were to view the play *Our American Cousin.*

During the third act Abraham took the hand of his wife. "What will Miss Harris think?" Mary asked. "She won't think anything about it," Lincoln replied. Those were his last words. John Wilkes Booth, an actor and a Southern sympathizer who had called slavery a blessing for blacks, stepped into the President's box. He placed a derringer at the back of Lincoln's head and pulled the trigger. As Lincoln slumped forward Booth jumped from the box. His spur caught in a Treasury Department flag, causing him to break his leg when he hit the stage. Always the actor, Booth shouted, *"Sic semper tyrannis"*—Thus always to tyrants—before he fled.

Lincoln was carried across the street to the house of William Petersen. His tall form was laid diagonally on a simple bed in a small first-floor bedroom. Attending physicians knew there was no hope; the bullet had lodged deep in Lincoln's brain. The Cabinet, with the exception of Secretary of State Seward, who had been wounded in the same assassination plot, gathered around their stricken president.

As Lincoln's breathing slowed and his color faded, Mary Lincoln's mind and body could no longer bear the unbearable. Two sons dead, and now her beloved husband lying mortally wounded before her. A physician ordered Mary from the room. Abraham Lincoln died at 7:22 A.M. on April 15, 1865. Secretary of War Edwin Stanton is reported to have said, "Now he belongs to the Ages."

Heartened by the Union's military victories, Lincoln gave his Second Inaugural Address "with high hopes for the future." In the address he spoke of the irony that both sides "read the same Bible, and pray to the same God." He pondered the unforeseen length of the war and explained it by saying: "The Almighty has his own purposes." Perhaps "God wills that it continue . . . until every drop of blood drawn with the lash, shall be paid by another drawn with the sword." He closed with certainty and compassion.

With malice toward none; with charity for all; with firmness in the right, as God gives us to see the right, let us strive on to finish the work we are in; to bind up the nation's wounds; to care for him who shall have borne the battle, and for his widow and his orphan—to do all which may achieve and cherish a just and lasting peace, among ourselves, and with all nations.

Abraham Lincoln was enjoying the play "Our American Cousin," a comedy, the night John Wilkes Booth killed him. Today Ford's Theatre presents plays ranging from Shakespeare to musicals.

PAT JOHNSON

Booth's diary.

PAT JOHNSON

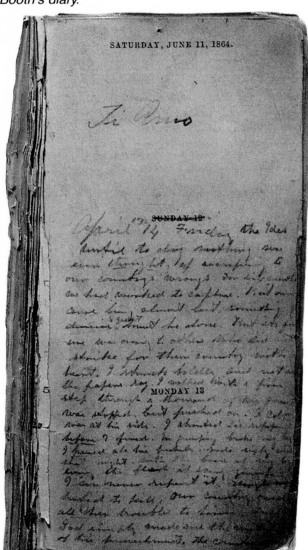

The derringer.

PAT JOHNSON

Born in a log cabin, Abraham Lincoln died in the rented bedroom of a clerk. Although his death was attended by the famous and his works were heralded by many, this did not lessen his family's grief.

PAT JOHNSON

The Mystery Portrait of Abraham Lincoln

Walt Whitman never met Abraham Lincoln, though he saw him many times. Whitman was impressed with Lincoln's appearance but was troubled that "None of the artists or pictures has caught the deep, though subtle and indirect expression of this man's face." Whitman's observation holds true to this day. Not one of the hundreds of portraits and photographs of Lincoln seems to reveal the genius, the humor, the compassion of the man we know from his writings.

All that changed for me one day while I was doing research at one of the great Lincoln repositories, the Louis A. Warren Lincoln Library and Museum in Fort Wayne, Indiana. In one of the files I came upon a color lithograph that stopped me in my tracks. *"This,"* I thought, "is the Lincoln I know."

The library staff provided me with their background file on the lithograph. Instead of finding answers, however, I discovered a mystery unsolved to this day. According to numerous clippings and publications, the original painting on which the lithograph was based was purchased by Chester H. Kunning for $35 at a Columbus, Ohio, antique shop in 1932.

As Kunning tells the story, he had the unsigned painting examined by various art critics and museum directors. They declared it the work of poet and painter Thomas Buchanan Read. From his research Kunning claims he discovered the following history of the painting.

In 1864 Read and Lincoln were guests at the same house in Washington, D.C. Read took this rare opportunity to do a quick portrait of the President on one of the 8″ x 10″ wooden panels the artist carried to do field sketches of the Civil War. After completing a sketch, the artist normally took the panels back to his studio, where he transferred the scene to canvas. In this case the hosts were so impressed with the painting that Read gave it to them as a gift. It was then handed down through the family until it ended up in the Columbus antique shop.

The painting, promoted by Kunning, attracted a great deal of enthusiastic attention. Some Lincoln scholars declared it the greatest likeness ever of the sixteenth president. Articles on it were run in many publications, including the *New York Times*, the *Chicago Tribune*, and *The Saturday Evening Post*. The original painting was displayed to eager crowds in the Illinois Host House at the 1932 Chicago World's Fair. During the 1930s both a black-and-white print and the color lithograph that began this story were widely sold.

Where is this original painting today? In 1978 as Mr. Kunning lay dying of Parkinson's disease he said it was in the Louis A. Warren Library and Museum. However, while the library does have copies of the color lithograph, they have never had the original painting. Is the painting by Thomas Buchanan Read? Perhaps, but another portrait of Lincoln known to be by Read was executed in an entirely different style. Does the painting, whoever the artist, capture a side of Lincoln not yet touched? The answer to that seems to be an unqualified "Yes."   L.W.

Located in Fort Wayne, Indiana, the Louis A. Warren Lincoln Library and Museum is one of the great Lincoln repositories. The museum features 60 displays that portray the life and accomplishments of our sixteenth president. The library houses 10,000 volumes and 6,000 prints on the Lincoln theme. The facility is funded by the Lincoln National Life Insurance Company.

SCOTT SIMPSON, COURTESY LOUIS A. WARREN LINCOLN LIBRARY & MUSEUM

The Lincoln Legacy

The country survived Abraham Lincoln's death. For Mary Lincoln, however, the loss was almost too great to bear. Always susceptible to depression, and overcome with grief, she lay in her room at the White House, unable to attend her husband's funeral or even descend the stairs to the East Room, where his body lay in state.

After a month Mary was finally able to pack, taking with her 60 crates containing her family's lifetime possessions. Some people accused her of looting the White House, and barren rooms seemed to support their accusations. Most of the missing items, though, had been taken by intruders as Mary lay helpless. At first friends had stood by in the White House to comfort her; later they shied away from the darkness of her all-encompassing grief.

Mary, Tad, and Robert settled in Chicago. At first Mary referred to their residence as a "hotel"; later she downgraded it to a "boarding house." Grief and hopelessness were overcoming her. Writing to Elizabeth Keckley, her black seamstress from the White House days, Mary confessed, "I am positively dying with a broken heart, and the probability is that I shall be living but a very short time. May we all meet in a better world." Concerning a debt, Mary wrote, "Do go, dear Lizzie, and implore them to be moderate, for I am in a very narrow place." Mary lost her confidante and "best living friend" when Elizabeth published a ghostwritten autobiography detailing her friendship with Mrs. Lincoln. Mary felt betrayed, and she never wrote to Elizabeth again.

Lincoln's widow also felt betrayed by her country. Troubled by her reputation for extravagance, Congress was slow to grant her a pension. Newspapers condemned her spending habits. Finally, in 1868 Mary fled to Europe, where, she told acquaintances, she was going to receive medical treatment and live more cheaply. In truth, she

could not bear the memories and the maliciousness.

Shortly after Mary Lincoln returned from Europe in 1871, Tad died. Mary wrote, "I have been prostrated by illness—& by a grief—that the grave alone can soften." But she had yet another indignity to suffer. In 1875, after consulting with friends and physicians, Robert had a court commit his

MATHEW BRADY—LLOYD OSTENDORF

In death Lincoln returned to Springfield, Illinois. The Lincoln Tomb at Oak Ridge Cemetery also holds the remains of Mary Todd Lincoln and three of the Lincolns' four sons. Robert Todd Lincoln is buried in Arlington National Cemetery.

Mary Todd Lincoln was a proud and loving woman. The more fate took from her, the more she tried to hold fast to what was left.

JEFF GNASS

mother to a mental institution. She was released the next year and eventually moved to her sister's home in Springfield. Mary lay alone in a darkened bedroom just as she had years before in her own Springfield home. There she had waited out her migraine headaches so that she could once again join her husband. When she rejoined her husband this time, on July 16, 1882, her misery would never return.

Robert Lincoln led a more productive life after his father's death than did his mother. He became a successful Chicago lawyer. Eventually he was appointed Secretary of War by President James Garfield; and in 1889 President Benjamin Harrison appointed him minister to England. After leav-

ing public life Robert became president of the Pullman Car Company.

In 1868 Robert had married Mary Eunice Harlan; they had three children: Mary, Abraham, and Jessie. Mary had a son, Lincoln Isham. Jessie had two children, Mary Lincoln Beckwith and Robert Todd Lincoln Beckwith. Robert Beckwith, the last direct descendant of Abraham Lincoln, died at 81 on Christmas Eve, 1985.

Although Abraham Lincoln's bloodline has ended, his legacy has not. In his first term as president he became increasingly convinced that the constitution needed an amendment to abolish slavery. That would finish the work the Emancipation Proclamation had begun. The Thirteenth

BY THE PRESIDENT OF THE UNITED STATES OF AMERICA.

A Proclamation.

Whereas, on the twenty-second day of September, in the year of our Lord one thousand eight hundred and sixty-two, a proclamation was issued by the President of the United States, containing, among other things, the following, to wit:

"That on the first day of January, in the year of our Lord one thousand eight hundred and sixty-three, all persons held as slaves within any State or designated part of a State, the people whereof shall then be in rebellion against the United States, shall be then, thenceforward, and forever, free; and the Executive government of the United States, including the military and naval authority thereof, will recognize and maintain the freedom of such persons, and will do no act or acts to repress such persons, or any of them, in any efforts they may make for their actual freedom.

"That the Executive will, on the first day of January aforesaid, by proclamation, designate the States and parts of States, if any, in which the people thereof, respectively, shall then be in rebellion against the United States; and the fact that any State, or the people thereof, shall on that day be in good faith represented in the Congress of the United States, by members chosen thereto at elections wherein a majority of the qualified voters of such State shall have participated, shall, in the absence of strong countervailing testimony, be deemed conclusive evidence that such State, and the people thereof, are not then in rebellion against the United States."

Now, therefore, I, ABRAHAM LINCOLN, PRESIDENT OF THE UNITED STATES, by virtue of the power in me vested as commander-in-chief of the army and navy of the United States, in time of actual armed rebellion against the authority and government of the United States, and as a fit and necessary war measure for suppressing said rebellion, do, on this first day of January, in the year of our Lord one thousand eight hundred and sixty-three, and in accordance with my purpose so to do, publicly proclaimed for the full period of one hundred days from the day first above mentioned, order and designate as the States and parts of States wherein the people thereof, respectively, are this day in rebellion against the United States, the following, to wit: ARKANSAS, TEXAS, LOUISIANA, (except the Parishes of St. Bernard, Plaquemines, Jefferson, St. John, St. Charles, St. James, Ascension, Assumption, Terre Bonne, Lafourche, St. Mary, St. Martin, and Orleans, including the City of New Orleans,) MISSISSIPPI, ALABAMA, FLORIDA, GEORGIA, SOUTH CAROLINA, NORTH CAROLINA, AND VIRGINIA, (except the forty-eight counties designated as West Virginia, and also the counties of Berkeley, Accomac, Northampton, Elizabeth City, York, Princess Ann, and Norfolk, including the cities of Norfolk and Portsmouth,) and which excepted parts are for the present left precisely as if this proclamation were not issued.

And by virtue of the power and for the purpose aforesaid, I do order and declare that all persons held as slaves within said designated States and parts of States are and henceforward shall be free; and that the Executive government of the United States, including the military and naval authorities thereof, will recognize and maintain the freedom of said persons.

And I hereby enjoin upon the people so declared to be free to abstain from all violence, unless in necessary self-defence; and I recommend to them that, in all cases when allowed, they labor faithfully for reasonable wages.

And I further declare and make known that such persons, of suitable condition, will be received into the armed service of the United States, to garrison forts, positions, stations, and other places, and to man vessels of all sorts in said service.

And upon this act, sincerely believed to be an act of justice warranted by the Constitution upon military necessity, I invoke the considerate judgment of mankind and the gracious favor of Almighty God.

In witness whereof I have hereunto set my hand and caused the seal of the United States to be affixed.

[L. S.]   Done at the CITY OF WASHINGTON this first day of January, in the year of our Lord one thousand eight hundred and sixty-three, and of the Independence of the United States of America the eighty-seventh.

By the President: *Abraham Lincoln*

William H. Seward, Secretary of State.

A true copy, with the autograph signatures of the President and the Secretary of State.

Jno. G. Nicolay,
Priv. Sec. to the President.

BOB DAUM

Historian and Lincoln authority Mark E. Neely, Jr., considers the Emancipation Proclamation "the equal of the Declaration of Independence in significance for the history of this country." Because Lincoln based the proclamation on military law, it freed slaves only in those areas controlled by the Confederates. The news of the Emancipation was enthusiastically received by slaves throughout the country, however. It set the stage for the Thirteenth Amendment to the Constitution and an end forever to the "hateful institution."

Amendment resolution was passed by Congress, then signed by Lincoln on February 1, 1865. During the remaining ten weeks of his life, 20 states ratified the amendment. On December 18, 1865, ratification by the necessary three-fourths majority of states was obtained. President Lincoln had always idolized the framers of the Constitution; now he joined them.

The abolishment of slavery and the preservation of the Union were Abraham Lincoln's two major public concerns and are his two principal accomplishments. Far more of his speeches and letters were devoted to these subjects than to any others. His term as our country's president still casts a broad shadow over the rest of our nation's history. Historians sit on scholarly panels and debate the influence and meaning of his life. Cities and banks, restaurants and children's toys bear his name. (When Lincoln was asked whether Lincoln County, Illinois, had been named after him he joked, "Well, it was named after I was.")

Abraham Lincoln's stature as president is so great that all subsequent chief executives have evoked his name. Harry Truman, for example, compared his own dealings with General Douglas McArthur with Lincoln's dealings with General George McClellan. Lyndon Johnson asserted, "Abraham Lincoln abolished slavery, and we can abolish poverty." On August 16, 1971, at the dedication of Lincoln Home National Historic site, President Richard Nixon said of Lincoln, "He was a very competitive man. . . . He lost elections, and came back to win for the Presidency of the United States. He never gave up."

The Lincoln Home is just one of many National Park Service areas that present the story of Abraham Lincoln. The Lincoln Monument Association was commissioned two years after his death, but it was not until 1914 that work began on a Lincoln Memorial in Washington, D.C. Architect Henry Bacon patterned the memorial after the Parthenon in Greece. Inside is a 19-foot seated statue of Lincoln by sculptor Daniel Chester French. Both the statue and the memorial are carved from Colorado marble. The memorial contains 36 columns representing the 36 states in Lincoln's union. Carved in stone on the walls are the words from his two most eloquent speeches: the Gettysburg Address and the Second Inaugural Address.

On May 30, 1922, the Lincoln Memorial was dedicated. Many dignitaries were present, including Chief Justice of the Supreme Court William Howard Taft and President Warren G. Harding. Also present were some who had known the

At times man's creativity soars to great heights. In the Lincoln Memorial architect Henry Bacon and sculptor Daniel Chester French have given us a memorial that is indeed worthy of our sixteenth president.

JEFF GNASS

Great Emancipator, including his son Robert Todd Lincoln.

Across town are two less imposing structures that also serve as memorials to Abraham Lincoln: Ford's Theatre and the House Where Lincoln Died. Shortly after the assassination, businessman John T. Ford wanted to stage plays in his theatre again. A public outcry arose, and the War Department ordered the building closed. To satisfy Ford they paid him $1,500 a month in rent. In 1866 the War Department purchased the building and turned it into offices for the U.S. Record and Pension Bureau.

In 1893 death again visited Ford's Theatre. All three floors collapsed during working hours, killing 22 employees. The building was repaired and used for offices until 1928, when it was transferred to the Office of Public Buildings and Public Parks of the National Capital. In 1933 Ford's Theatre became part of the national park system, and in 1964 Congress appropriated over $2 million to restore Ford's Theatre to its appearance in Lincoln's era. In February 1968 Ford's Theatre began presentation of *John Brown's Body,* a play about the causes of the Civil War—the first production at Ford's Theatre since the night of April 14, 1865.

Gettysburg National Military Park was also transferred from the War Department to the National Park Service in 1933. Although there are 26 National Park Service areas commemorating events of the Civil War, Gettysburg stands apart. It was here, in the "high water mark" of the Confederacy, that General Lee directed his troops against the center of the Union forces on Cemetery Ridge. Pickett's Charge was turned back, and with it, the hopes of the Confederacy. It was here also that President Abraham Lincoln came to pay tribute to the "honored dead" of Gettysburg in

45

This was Lincoln's Cabinet room, where on July 22, 1862, he read the Emancipation Proclamation to his assembled Cabinet members. Today the room is furnished with pieces from the Lincoln period. Mrs. Lincoln had purchased the bed in 1861 for a guest room.

WHITE HOUSE HISTORICAL ASSOCIATION

his simple yet eloquent words.

The White House was home not only to Abraham Lincoln but also to all American presidents except George Washington. Lincoln's presence here remains substantial. His portrait hangs in the State Dining Room and the modern Cabinet Room. Lincoln's own Cabinet Room, where he pondered over the Civil War and signed the Emancipation Proclamation, is now the Lincoln Bedroom, appointed with furniture from Lincoln's time. The White House, too, became part of the national park system in 1933.

Lincoln's rise from a log cabin to the White House is part of his mystique. In 1904 a group of famous Americans including Mark Twain and William Jennings Bryan formed the Lincoln Farm Association to save Lincoln's birthplace in Kentucky. By 1905 the association had collected enough donations to buy the farm near Hodgenville. The next year they were able to buy a log cabin, moved from the site in 1860, that possibly contained logs from the Lincoln cabin. With this accomplished, the association began a public campaign for a memorial building to cover and protect the cabin. Money poured in, including pennies from school children, and in 1911 the memorial was dedicated. The memorial became a national park in 1916 and was placed under the

jurisdiction of the War Department. In 1933 it was transferred to the National Park Service, and 1959 was redesignated as a national historic site.

SUGGESTED READING

BASLER, ROY P., ed. *Abraham Lincoln: His Speeches and Writings.* [1946] New York: Grosset & Dunlap, 1962.

DUFF, JOHN J. *A. Lincoln: Prairie Lawyer.* New York: Rinehart & Company, 1960.

HERNDON, WILLIAM H. and JESSE W. WEIK. *Herndon's Life of Lincoln.* [1889] Angle, Paul M., ed. New York: Da Capo Press, Inc., 1983.

LORANT, STEFAN. *Lincoln: A Picture Story of His Life.* [1952] New York: W. W. Norton, 1969.

NEELY, MARK E. *The Abraham Lincoln Encyclopedia.* New York: McGraw-Hill Book Company, 1982.

OATES, STEPHEN B. *With Malice Toward None: The Life of Abraham Lincoln.* New York: Harper and Row, 1977.

RANDALL, RUTH P. *Mary Lincoln: Biography of a Marriage.* Boston: Little, Brown and Company, 1953.

SANDERS, GERALD. *Abraham Lincoln Fact Book.* Philadelphia: Eastern Acorn Press, 1982.

THOMAS, BENJAMIN P. *Abraham Lincoln.* New York: Alfred A. Knopf, 1952.

———. *Lincoln's New Salem.* Springfield: The Abraham Lincoln Association, 1934.

WARREN, LOUIS A. *Lincoln's Youth: Indiana Years, Seven to Twenty-one, 1816–1830.* Indianapolis: Indiana Historical Society, 1959.

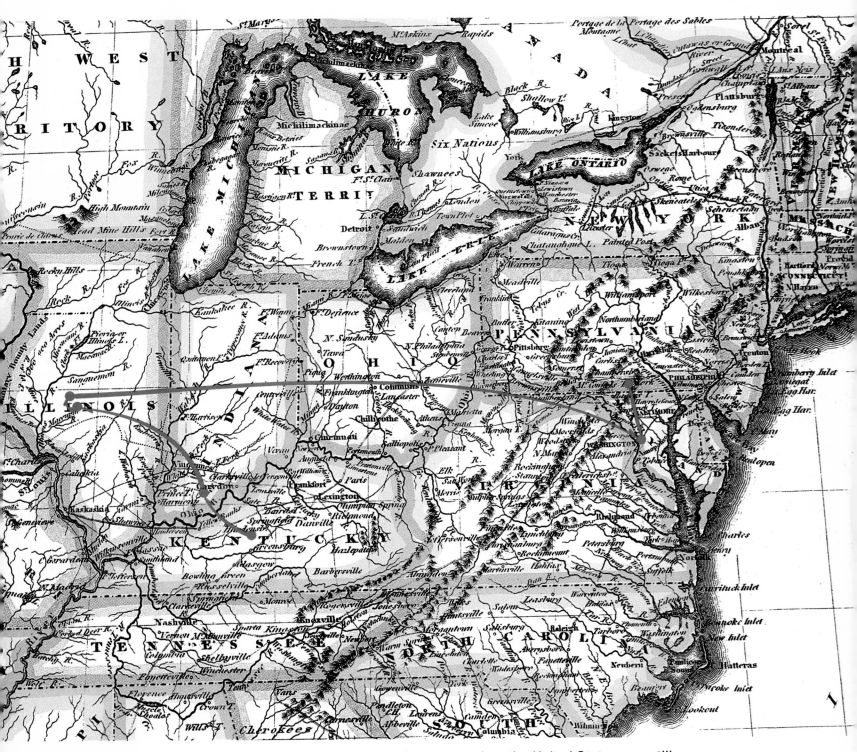

Abraham Lincoln lived during the first half of the nineteenth century, when the United States was still an emerging nation. Lewis and Clark had recently opened a route to the Pacific Northwest, and Illinois was virtually on the western boundary of our country.

The above map, "Corrected & Improved from the best Authorities," was published in 1820. At that time there were 26 states and 3 territories. Most of the place names refer to rivers, as these waterways provided one of the principal means of transportation and commerce.

Where Lincoln was born, grew to manhood, and lived until he was elected president was essentially a frontier region. From humble beginnings in western Kentucky, Abe Lincoln moved on to southern Indiana and then to central Illinois, where he spent about half his life. The qualities of character he developed in the 52 years he spent in these states served him well, for he became one of our greatest, if not the greatest, of our presidents.

First efforts to preserve the site of Lincoln's Indiana years began with concern over his mother's grave. In 1879 a half acre was donated to Spencer County, and a headstone was placed on Nancy Hanks Lincoln's grave. Later, through the efforts of the Indiana Lincoln Union and other groups, the Nancy Hanks Lincoln State Memorial was created. In 1962, 114 acres that included the grave of Lincoln's mother were donated to the federal government to be administered as Lincoln Boyhood National Memorial. At this site the National Park Service now operates a farm where schoolchildren can perform the same chores the Lincoln family did.

The only house that Abraham Lincoln ever owned was in Springfield, Illinois. After the assassination Mary Lincoln signed over her rights in the home to her sons Robert and Tad. When Tad died, Robert assumed sole ownership. He rented the house to a series of tenants until 1887, when he donated it to the state of Illinois. In 1971 the administration of the site was taken over by the National Park Service.

It is uncommon to have so many parks dedicated to the memory of one man. But then, Lincoln was common man with uncommon traits. Denied the opportunity for much schooling, he taught himself to read and write. Having chosen a profession suspected of placing pragmatism above honesty, he advised law students that if "you can not be an honest lawyer, resolve to be honest without being a lawyer." Faced with the choice of compromising his beliefs in equal rights for all men or preserving the Union, he held both dear. That the Union holds Abraham Lincoln dear is clearly demonstrated by the Lincoln National Parks.

A young child (left) gazes on the face of the Great Emancipator.

JEFF GNASS

Inside back cover: The Gettysburg Address at the Lincoln Memorial. Photo by Jeff Gnass.

Back Cover: Wagon at Lincoln Boyhood National Memorial. Photo by Bob Daum.

Printed by the Krueger Co.
Separations by Village Graphics
Typography by Stanley Stillion

Books in this series: Acadia, Alcatraz Island, Arches, Blue Ridge Parkway, Bryce Canyon, Canyon de Chelly, Cape Cod, Capitol Reef, Channel Islands, Civil War Parks, Crater Lake, Death Valley, Denali, Dinosaur, Everglades, Fort Clatsop, Gettysburg, Glen Canyon–Lake Powell, Grand Canyon, Grand Teton, Great Smoky Mountains, Haleakala, Hawaii Volcanoes, Lake Mead–Hoover Dam, Lincoln Parks, Mount Rainier, Mount Rushmore, Mount St. Helens, Olympic, Petrified Forest, Rocky Mountain, Sequoia–Kings Canyon, Scotty's Castle, Shenandoah, Statue of Liberty, Theodore Roosevelt, Virgin Islands, Yellowstone, Yosemite, Zion

Published by KC Publications · Box 14883 · Las Vegas, NV 89114